# CONFLICTED

# CONFLICTED

## A LITERARY ALBUM

Decipher James

*Conflicted*

Copyright © 2019 by Decipher James. All rights reserved.

---

No part of this publication may be reproduced, stored in a retrieval system or transmitted in any way by any means, electronic, mechanical, photocopy, recording or otherwise without the prior permission of the author except as provided by USA copyright law.

# CONTENTS

Preface . . . . . . . . . . . . . . . . . . . . . . . . . . . . . . . . . . . . . . . . . 7
The Birth. . . . . . . . . . . . . . . . . . . . . . . . . . . . . . . . . . . . . . . 9
Growth . . . . . . . . . . . . . . . . . . . . . . . . . . . . . . . . . . . . . . . 10
Russian Love . . . . . . . . . . . . . . . . . . . . . . . . . . . . . . . . . . 11
God's Gift . . . . . . . . . . . . . . . . . . . . . . . . . . . . . . . . . . . . 12
Value . . . . . . . . . . . . . . . . . . . . . . . . . . . . . . . . . . . . . . . . 14
Almost. . . . . . . . . . . . . . . . . . . . . . . . . . . . . . . . . . . . . . . 16
Tragedy . . . . . . . . . . . . . . . . . . . . . . . . . . . . . . . . . . . . . . 17
Fearful Tears . . . . . . . . . . . . . . . . . . . . . . . . . . . . . . . . . . 18
Black Coffee . . . . . . . . . . . . . . . . . . . . . . . . . . . . . . . . . . 19
Undefined . . . . . . . . . . . . . . . . . . . . . . . . . . . . . . . . . . . .20
Just For you . . . . . . . . . . . . . . . . . . . . . . . . . . . . . . . . . . .21
Overthinking. . . . . . . . . . . . . . . . . . . . . . . . . . . . . . . . . .22
One Time Lover . . . . . . . . . . . . . . . . . . . . . . . . . . . . . . .24
Freed . . . . . . . . . . . . . . . . . . . . . . . . . . . . . . . . . . . . . . . .25
Free Appeal . . . . . . . . . . . . . . . . . . . . . . . . . . . . . . . . . . .26
Sunrise. . . . . . . . . . . . . . . . . . . . . . . . . . . . . . . . . . . . . . .27
I want to See You. . . . . . . . . . . . . . . . . . . . . . . . . . . . . .29
Peace of mind . . . . . . . . . . . . . . . . . . . . . . . . . . . . . . . . .31
Do you? . . . . . . . . . . . . . . . . . . . . . . . . . . . . . . . . . . . . .32
Love Hate . . . . . . . . . . . . . . . . . . . . . . . . . . . . . . . . . . . .34
Morning Dew . . . . . . . . . . . . . . . . . . . . . . . . . . . . . . . .36

Bloom . . . . . . . . . . . . . . . . . . . . . . . . . . . . . . . . . . . . . .37
Seeded Love . . . . . . . . . . . . . . . . . . . . . . . . . . . . . . . . .38
Lust . . . . . . . . . . . . . . . . . . . . . . . . . . . . . . . . . . . . . . . .39
Measure of A Man . . . . . . . . . . . . . . . . . . . . . . . . . . . .41
Pure Love Child . . . . . . . . . . . . . . . . . . . . . . . . . . . . . .42
Honey . . . . . . . . . . . . . . . . . . . . . . . . . . . . . . . . . . . . . .43
Final Spark . . . . . . . . . . . . . . . . . . . . . . . . . . . . . . . . . .44
Healing Waters . . . . . . . . . . . . . . . . . . . . . . . . . . . . . . .46
The Outro. . . . . . . . . . . . . . . . . . . . . . . . . . . . . . . . . . .48
The End . . . . . . . . . . . . . . . . . . . . . . . . . . . . . . . . . . . .49
Notes. . . . . . . . . . . . . . . . . . . . . . . . . . . . . . . . . . . . . . .50
Notes. . . . . . . . . . . . . . . . . . . . . . . . . . . . . . . . . . . . . . .51
Notes. . . . . . . . . . . . . . . . . . . . . . . . . . . . . . . . . . . . . . .52
Notes. . . . . . . . . . . . . . . . . . . . . . . . . . . . . . . . . . . . . . .53

# PREFACE

I wrote this leaving out most of the punctuation to give anyone that reads a chance to interpret the pieces however they may please. I know what each one is supposed to mean and sound like, but people hear and read things the way they want so I just made it easy. This is my first, so it will probably be the most imperfect work of art that I've ever made but this needed to be created. Take the term literary album and give it whatever definition you feel fit but, this is mine. I don't really hope this will create some form of understanding but, I hope the words resonate. Thank you to everyone and everything that has ever inspired me to write. I appreciate more than I can probably ever express.

# THE BIRTH

I am a sun child
Born in darkness
Bred from everything beautiful in the world
Don't take this as vanity
When I look inside I see all the broken
pieces that became of me
Shamelessly
Growing past the past
Addressing all the shortcomings
Towards a future of forward thinking steadfast
I'm the last king of my lineage
I have been blessed with hope to breed
another free to express and flow
I will not pass my past nor my present
I will pass on my future in a manner of patient reverence
These growing pains may be unpleasant
All to manifest the truest destiny.

# GROWTH

My deepest lust in life is growth
I fiend for it
Whatever it looks like
It's no longer in a form that can be measured
by rulers or marks on a wall
It's no longer measured by the mastering
of subjects that you'll never use
That somehow gives a metric of intelligence
that the world takes as gospel
I want to learn as much as I want to teach
I think god is teaching me patience by
giving the keys piece by piece
I want it all at once
But that may not be the remedy for me.

# RUSSIAN LOVE

Like water rushes, thoughts of you rushing to my temple
Penetrating my temple
Throwing off my usual tempo
I'd like to think that this was incidental
Accidents happen but at this moment I think you meant to
Leave me with a momenta
Of you
Of your love
Of your feeling
Of your smell
Of your aura
I think we should just feel it
We don't have to go in order
We don't have to be numerical
We don't have to follow traditions made in America
Let's make love great again
Being inside your presence better than
sliding through DMs on Instagram
Ironically that lead us here
In the moment I wasn't ready I'll blame that on fear
And That's okay I probably would've messed it up
But with perfect timing you're my perfect blessing love.

# GOD'S GIFT

I think God gave you to me
Not like to own
But to have and to hold until we both grow old
I think God gave you to me
Laid you right in my lap
Is this a ruse
God how could you choose to give me
something beautiful as that
Lord Knows I got butter fingers but
somehow I was able to catch
You
It was unexpected
If I recollect it
From the moment I saw you, you were in my heart.
Through self-reflection
Let's leave the past in the past and
focus on future introspection
Self-Surrender
And blend it with fruits of the spirit that
make a shake of love never ending
Never Failing
I'm not prepared but through God we can get anywhere
I'm aware that this is new to us
This metamorphosis from lust to love
And its deep
Way below the surface
I promise to help you manifest your purpose

I promise to give you the love you deserve
I promise to put you first
And if we get lost
I promise to climb mountains cross rivers and seas to meet you right back where our love needs to be.

# VALUE

Intrinsic Value is powerful
I could go on for hours about how you should value you
It's electric to feed yourself self-confidence too
Force Feed all the self's that you need
Trapped in your heart is worst kind
of bondage I've ever seen
Frozen like night terrors when the answer
is clear to everyone but we
We the people
Strive to dig deeper and deeper
To know thyself is to know great wealth
Be in tune with nature and all your features
Never be someone else featuring you
Be the star to the steal the show
Be the you you never show
Glow until your light blinds everything
that shouldn't be present
There's a purpose for your presence
Find it then lend it
But don't bend to conformity
You were born with a uniqueness
Our differences and similarities are
seeds to the trees of unity
Create in me a clean heart
At least a clean part
So giving of myself won't seem like a chore that's so hard

Please don't bar yourself inside a prison
Life was made to make mistakes only
way to avoid them is not to live it
True wealth is loving yourself and doing it richly
I woke up this morning to find this epiphany.

# ALMOST

I almost lost you
Almost slipped through my grips
Almost became the last time I felt the warmth of your kiss
All that being said I think I'd be remiss to dismiss whatever
feeling I put aside to even fathom creating this divide
If I could speak plain
I could feel the pain and hurt in your voice
And I cried because what I imagined to be
easy was 3 more than a difficult choice
Will you still love me in the end
When all the flowers have bloomed
And your just as consumed as I by your external
beauty and that which lies within
I pray that you will
I pray fate takes the wheel
Cross my heart and hope to die so you know it's real.

# TRAGEDY

Good Morning Woman
I'm a broken man
Trying to put the pieces back together in this broken land
Shedding all the layers of toxic masculinity
And sharing all the love I have is my triumphant stand
I can
I can be vulnerable
I can be strong
I can lead
I can be a father to our seed
I know
I know hurt
I know pain
I know tears
I know Love
It wasn't a dream but it's the love I know
I hope you're the answer to my nightmares and fears
I hope we cry enough tears of happiness
to fill the ocean blue times 3
Seal this pact with a kiss
My Juliet
My Cleopatra
My Lover my queen
Let's close our eyes and jump
Loving without reservation is my favorite tragedy.

# FEARFUL TEARS

I cried to you
I cried for you
I cried
Like a baby, you held me close and
wiped the tears from my eyes
In that moment you couldn't have pried
my arms from you if you tried
In that moment I felt too vulnerable to look you in the eyes
In that moment your bosom was the only
place comfortable enough to hide….

I've always thought the word bosom was hilarious from the first time I read it in the bible. I just knew I had to use it in a poem one day. Thank you for giving me that opportunity love. That was probably one of the most vulnerable moments I've ever shared with a person and I don't take any of it as a joke. I almost had this printed without clarifying that.

# BLACK COFFEE

Those lips
The ones between your hips and the ones that I kiss
That might've left something to thought
So I'll try to be a little more specific
The lips underneath your nose that I kiss and curl your toes
So gorgeously thick we kiss I grow and your water flows
I love to feel your warm sensation
Your moaning is laced with the most beautiful sex faces
I'm glad to be facing you
Can't help but focus on you
At attention my mission is to give you all my inches
I hope you'll approve
We're soon to be
Partners in this lustful monogamy
Please trust that I aim to please
Spread your legs as I creep in between
Aim at that velvet center till everything in you feels free
Studied your anatomy and its my pleasure
to bring you to your peak
This mountain top is therapy
This pillow talk is chemistry
I think we're balanced chemically.

# UNDEFINED

I don't think love was ever meant to be binary
Lines of ones and zeros could never
do our love story justice
I love when it's just us
I never understood why they called it caked up
Probably has something to do with love being sweet
They'd probably think we were bland if they didn't know us
You know me and I know you
You renewed my belief in trust
Alienated my need for lust
I must give it up to you
My money and my cars
Flowers cards and candy
I'm fortunate to have met you at the
perfect time and the perfect shape
A mango season ago all I had to give was headaches
I'm here to face all my uncertainties
You've given me something so precious.

# JUST FOR YOU

I don't believe that this is poetic but
it may be in that it is true
It took a while to write because I didn't know if
there were enough words to describe this truth
You are optimistic you are vulnerable you are powerful
You are a flower who's bloomed on
so many different occasions
In a word it might be flowerful
So amazed
In a daze to your matchless glow
You yearn for growth in all the things you lack to know
You've taken your scars and used them to float
You've lost sight of your dream and reeled in the rope
You are hope for a better love
You are inquisitive
Your lust to live is a gift worth more
than any other can give
Queen of hearts you've shown all your cards
And the hand that you've dealt is enough
to battle any and all odds
Please don't question this
Just reference it when things become uncomfortably hard
You're a constellation pouring out tears
that show that you want more
Let your frustration be the catalyst to reach the
untapped portions of this galaxy you seek to explore
Through this journey I'll only love you more.

# OVERTHINKING

I think
I think
I think too much
I need to react
Consistently
I think I used to drink too much
I slowed it down because you said I wouldn't listen
Or I'd go missing
Call my phone and accuse me of
drowning in someone else's kisses
I'd lie and lay with you at night wishing
my conscience was different
I stink
I stink
I stink too much
I need a shower
To wash away the pain and the hurt I felt the last hour
Maybe the day
Week, month, maybe even a year
I could use a distraction
It's more attractive than facing your fears
Have no fear we're super heroes here
Holding in emotions without exploding
or even so much as a shear
Drop a tear for us
Plus a symbolic moment of silence
These hands of mine been built to grind
And all I need in this life of sin is a rider

Is a lifer to do life with me
Someone schedule oriented cause I only got a few
openings for appointments with emotional availability
Build with me baby my house is
broken but the door is open
I got plans but I'm rarely focused
Too busy hoping someone will save me with a hocus pocus
My stench is potent
I been thinking
Thoughts are overdosing
Please be the potion
Save me from me I'm drowning in this open ocean
You're the great hope
Can I drain you so I can focus
Here's my number just let me know….

# ONE TIME LOVER

I made love once
The most selfish thing I've ever done
Kind of ironic but its true because it
happened while I was numb
Mixed the liquor with the reefer
To dig in my feelings deeper
Cross faded the perfect concoction
that this moment would need
I guess by now you can tell that I didn't love her
She was cool but I was hurting
I'm sorry you didn't deserve it at all
Maybe I'm overreacting
You enjoyed the moment but there was a point
when I knew that I was in too deep
From the moment I started to kiss you as
if I loved you or if I missed you
It opened a box of emotions that I saw
in your eyes you could feel.
I'd apologize but would that really
make a change in our lives
Do I dare to open a wound that may
have already healed with time
Part of me solemnly swears to never take my
soul to a place where I'm so hurt I'll give the
love in my soul to any woman that's near
Have no fear I'm working on healing
The understanding of self is an appealing feeling.

# FREED

Free from bondage
A cage for love grows and shows
more than you'll ever know
Anything her heart desires she aspires to attain
Her lust for life is an everlasting flame
I'm not ashamed to say she was my muse
My accelerant the match and even the fuse
I don't know if it was a love story more
like a bomb I dare not diffuse
We were explosive and disruptive more
than five steps past destructive
Four steps past seductive
And 3 high off our own emissions
Purely addicting.

# FREE APPEAL

You appeal to a freer me
The part of me that loves more and thinks less
The part of me that childishly dismisses any
responsibility that may cause stress
The part of me that never guarantees or places bets
The part of me that loathes the mundane
of planning what to do next
You appeal to the conversations
about poetry over herbal tea
The words cascade from your lips and somehow
levitate to somewhere deep in me
You appeal to a simpler me
Prodigy of genuine freedom
I want to be free from the beliefs of normalcy
The traditional boundaries of monogamy
This part of me is committed to eliminating all the
definitive lines defined by the powers that be
Must I choose
Ironically I still can't have my cake and eat it too
I can't commit myself to stability and
still profess my soul to you
Freely roam this prison until I find
it inside myself to choose
Freedom
Freedom, with you.

# SUNRISE

I watched the sunrise with a cloaked goddess
She was modest
Her aura elevated my body
She was captivating
She captured every bit of my mind
As we sat there in the dark forgetting every essence of time
Her presence the most elegant refreshment
Reminiscent of younger days when love was
simple and ignorance blissfully lead the way
I wish we could stay
I should be sure that it's lust
The voice of a gorgeous siren dangerously
tempting me to touch
We don't need trust
Let's just feel in the moments before the
sun sheds light on our naïve narrative
It's imperative that I shake you off
But as the sun rises I find myself in indecision
As the waves whisper her words sweet ever the more
I considered myself a realist but in this moment
all those notions become no more.
No more thoughts of love in a box
An image forms of love so abstract and unorthodox
And its you

I had hoped the light would cause the illusion
in darkness to fade away but it enhanced
everything that her words had yet to say
I watched the sunrise with a cloaked goddess
Though we parted ways a piece of
her forever with me will stay.

# I WANT TO SEE YOU

I want to see you
Please don't leave me on read
For the first time that phrase isn't an invitation
for empty sexual favors in bed.
I want to see you
Your hopes that keep you driven
Your dreams so lucidly vivid
The fears that plague your mind
Know the strength in the tears that ache your heart
I want to see you
Feel your heartbeat against my chest
Sync your heart's beating with mine so I'll know
when you're at your worst and at your best.
When you're nervous or when you're scared
When confidence oozes through the pores of your skin
I'll know that feeling with you
I'll feel it so deep within
I want to see you
Let's slow dance to something like Marvin
I want more than a sexual healing
I want to feel total emotional involvement
With someone my heart and I are involved with
I want to feel us evolving
As the music creates a cloud
I see you in my arms nothing ever clearer than now
I want to see you
I hope by now you'll know what I mean

So many others have looked but won't
notice the details I've seen
Now that I see you
Everything feels so different
The soft caress of your lips feel like
drinking the sweetest elixir
Standing in front of you feels like
admiring a painted picture
Are you fictional
This novel so beautifully written
The pages drawing me close
The more I read the more we both seem to grow
Now that I see you
Look at you glow in the still of the night
Hershey brown sugar honey cinnamon drips off
your melanin skin when it hits the light
My queen, my lover, my partner in crime my peace of mind
Now that I see you
You ask what it's going to be
I'll give all my time for the peace of mind that
you'll work at making sure you see me.

# PEACE OF MIND

I suck at love and most of the things it's involved with
Still trying to find the switch so I can
turn on emotional involvement
Feels like I'm slowly evolving
Whether I like it is soon to come
I see the love in your eyes and my first reaction is to run
Like that gun you're holding is going to
shoot thru my heart instead of touch it
Been lost so long I'm confused by how gentle your touch is
Sun kissed born from milk and honey a
gorgeous orchid begins to bud
I feel like the lotus a symbol of peace
still trying to shake off the mud
I want peace of mind
You want a piece of mine to give it
Listen to this record play while these
candles burn and you'll hear it
Such a gorgeously rhythmic tone
Pillow talking my fantasies
The melody to this song
And if I knew what a soulmate was
X would mark the spot at you
Purity peace and love put together with golden glue
I got the flu
Please be my chicken noodle soup
Cliché but I could tell that you like corny and cute
In all serious I've had enough remedies I want the cure
To which you reply are you sure….

# DO YOU?

Do you really love me
Not a dime to my pocket
My hair nappy and ugly ambition and a dream minus
the dollar just wishing someone would hug me
Do you really love me
Why
Because I can't seem to see
I love what I see in the mirror
But do you love what you see in me
This love can't be surface deep
Peep
I may not be head of my household
But I'm pushing towards big goals
Shoes don't match with my clothes
Holes in the bottom of my soles
But my heart is pure
This world has shaped me but this one
pure heart might fuel the cure
Do you really love me
Enough to love all my flaws
Forget all my shortcomings I'm fighting against all odds
Odds are stacking up
While I seem to be running low
Real love is the real key to keeping this broken vessel whole
But do you really love me
Love us
Love we
Cause I haven't loved you right

I'll admit it ashamed but openly
But take my hand and show me how
to love because I'm willing
I want to learn and grow from you
Let's know each other let's build
But do I really love you
Sweetest lover of mine
When I put you inside a box so afraid
that you'll cross these lines
Break a barrier or two
Claiming it'll be okay instead of helping break barriers too
Do I really love you
With the way that I shape my words
My equal never my lesser
But less is all that is heard
As if less is what you deserve
Your strength is an inspiration
Your love can alter the world
But do I really love you
When your honor's at risk I'm lost
As if you're not worth fighting for if I
weigh the reward with the cost
Your love is priceless and I'll trade it all
Because I really love you
Put away all my reservations and reserve a love so true
Cause in this situation 1+1=1
And I only want to be 1 with you
Cause I really love you
You and only you.

# LOVE HATE

I'm everything that you love and everything that you hate
Something brought us together don't know if I'd call it fate
It's pretty debatable
Too worried about putting on for
societies standardized labels
You love that our thing is effortless hate that I never call
Never been one for tradition but as
the summer transitions to fall
Leaves you looking for definition
But if we define these blurred lines
will it ruin how we been living
You love after we make love I tell
you the things on my mind
You hate that when we cuddle I turn my back in the night
Who's to say that our thing is shallow they
don't know the things that we say
The pillows they hold our secrets until the next time we lay
And I would never play with you the honesty makes it real
And sometimes you hate that part
but love the raw sex appeal
Gazing in to your eyes surprised by the aggressive kissing
Laying out all the cards you know my artful intentions
Every Stroke a vital component to the masterpiece
She lets me know when it's done by
the weakness in her knees
You love the way that it feels you hate that we didn't wait
Time is always of essence you feel
like we put our love at stake

I know that we didn't force it the vibes took us away
Too late to rewind or hit replay
I'm everything that you love and everything that you hate
Love will always prevail let that tradition lead the way.

# MORNING DEW

I used to write about when it rained
slow my mind thinking rash
I hoped that I would find you in these lines
but, nothing good happens fast
So I sketched you out then made corrections
Until every piece of you was sweet perfection
My fantasy my beautiful blessing
No other would get my selection but you
Until I wrote another
Painting a mural with all these vibrant
colors and keeping it to myself
Fear that it wouldn't compare
Fear that I'd look in to the crowd and
catch the blankest of stares
Self-doubt is so cruel
Yet and still I told my soul through you
Every letter every word is true
So rain don't go away cause my words won't
come alive without the morning dew.

# BLOOM

Budding Flower your leaves are falling
You bloomed and the monsoons
brought the seasonal showers
The rains came drowning out all the enchanting hours
I'm a coward
Running away from something so
sweet used to it ending sour
If you I give you all I have will you stay till the final hour?

# SEEDED LOVE

Our love is a seed
Sprinkle water and let it grow
Kind Words are nutrients be sure to some of those flow
Along with hugs and kisses fertilizer for champs
If we make sure to communicate we
might just have ourselves a plant
Because seed I'm thinking about you
Will you be the rose with all the thorns
Or from this mysterious seed will
something beautiful be born
Seed I'm thinking about you
All things must come to an end
Could we grow old together
Or will we grow and divide at the stem
Seed I'm thinking about you
What ifs maybes and maybe not
Even when I'm away not a moment you leave my thoughts
That must mean something close to a lot
So seed I'll put my pride aside and love this
love with everything that I've got.

# LUST

If I mix love with lust what will I get
Two souls in opposite directions doomed to fail
Yearnings for love from a longing lack of affection
Finally someone sees her chaos
disguised as a needed blessing
So far from fate
A joining of energies is created
An apex of pain that leads to the most
passionate moments of insanity
Endless Strokes
Working to convince this narrative isn't wrong
The urge to fight back pressed up against the wall
Painting this perfect mural defenses begin to fall
And here they are vulnerable
Eyes comprised of truths
So their gaze never meets
In this moment two selfish fools
But the feel is deep sea
Breathing inside your neck each time it gets better
The feeling of her curves a highway lasting forever
Tasting her as their tongues write every letter
Knowing the truth but we choose not to do better
Love for someone else but lust brings us together
Can I build with you
Thoughts in a moment of mere distraction
Almost losing his way but the love pulls him back in
Does it really conquer all
Even lust

In these vile moments of passion love was
made that broke up the purest trust
Felt the warmth of a body whom these
hands shouldn't have touched
Is this costing too much
What's the total
Can love conquer that
Wash her off my body hope she never touches my heart
Trying hard to rewind my mind to death do us part
Stop and then press start.

# MEASURE OF A MAN

My deepest fear is to be incompetent
To lose my confidence
Starting to contradict what society defines as a man
Because somehow my vulnerability speaks on
my inability to succeed in leading a fam
Because somehow my tears and fears are symbols
of weakness instead of humility and meekness
Because I'm supposed to hide my oppression
My hard exterior my main tool of deflection when
it comes to expressing affection toward my queen
Descendants of royalty
I have not conquered lands but I've beat statistics
I have conquered stereotypes
Being swallowed by the darkness but being
strong enough to struggle to the light
A continuous fight
Still I am weak for wanting to share my soul with another
When I've shared a bed been in between legs
Shared my heart only to realize I've given
a part of myself to an empty cause
This is about me being consumed with gloom feeling
doomed to be one of the last deep thinkers alive
Endangered species too close to being
left behind but still I smile.

# PURE LOVE CHILD

A written symphony to the epiphany that love is blind
Love in immaculate hues blur these beautiful lines
All that is seen is warm colors of rhythm and blues
Passionate red desires a fire so well consumed
Blooms the rose from beneath all the ashes
byproduct of this natural disaster
Two hearts slowly begin to beat faster
Soon to fall in the unhappy pursuit of greener pastures
Feed us
Let patient love feed off a mind and time
A divine make up of matter
Our thoughts and selfless actions
make this love age like wine
In due time the cup will overflow
Spilling creating little pieces that'll be nurtured
to grow walk love listen and speak
Built to last the storm not to be sifted away like wheat
Sheets of melanin cover their skin
A shimmering glow surrounds them
exploding from deep within
Purity emitting its aura no evil can come from them
Pure love child.

# HONEY

Why let me be when this thing could be sweet as honey
Honey we could take it slow and if it feels right we
can build on it and make this honey comb grow
Who knows
I'm not afraid of your nectar
The substance in you makes the smallest things better
Don't worry I bring things to the table
besides flowers and love letters
We both know you won't settle
There's something special about you
In a different time and place I would've
found a reason to doubt you
Ready to love you like I lost you
I want to get lost in you
Some would say I'm a fool
Feels like I'm breaking laws to a game that has no rules
Building a house of love on solid ground and
as I go I'm learning which rules to use
Please don't abuse me for my lack of know
I know that I'll make mistakes I just hope
you love me through all the new growth
But this is only our verbal agreement so
I understand if you need to go
Just give me one last time to hold
you close then I'll let it be
Cause sometimes you gotta set the bees free
to see if honey comes back as sweet.

# FINAL SPARK

I know we said we were finished
And I know our spark is gone but I don't think
that our flame has really diminished
Pardon me but we have ourselves some unfinished business
This is supposed to be poetic but can we
fuck for the first time like it's our last
It is cause nothing good comes from digging in your past
If we're past that I apologize
Honestly no I don't
I want to feel the warmth of your
gorgeous insides I gotta know
I gotta know how you feel and see all your faces
Promise to take my time
Can't get it in for a minute that image just looks so wasteful
I hope we do it disgusting
I mean that being some kind of tasteful
Cause if this will only happen once I gotta embrace you
All of you
For as long as it's beautiful
Don't let that fool you in to thinking we're
making love this predicament is unusual
It's fruitful
Can we multiply
I caught the gaze in your eye
It took me to everywhere under the night sky
Maybe we should just shoot the breeze star
Or are we too far removed from our home
galaxy to make it back to these parts

Parts of you that really drive me crazy
Turn forever friends with benefits to forever my lady
And please have my babies
I been confused and missing you lately
That leads back to my initial question that
may have seemed more like a statement
Can we?
Shall we?
The first last time for you and me?
Then let it be?
Cause in my mind it was sour so this
moment is bound to be sweet.

# HEALING WATERS

She bathed me.
The simplicity of this action might lead the
factions, that have never had this happen to believe
that the magnitude of this was miniscule
The intimacy in this exchange is something
I haven't been able to explain and to this day
when I take showers I think of you.
She bathed me
Something so unexpected I remember feeling
every groove in her hands, and how the confusion
in my mind ran circles until I let go
Then I was yours
Fully submitted to you
As you scrubbed the dirt from my body the hurt the
frustration, and the self-doubt went with it too
Questioning what I did to deserve this
Was it something that I did, or said
That you would go and do something to
confuse every thought of you in my head
I think we both knew it wasn't love
But as the water trickled down my back
my defenses ran down the drain
And for these moments it felt like distant
lovers had found each other again
We'd gone so far
To the point that something I thought
was sexual was spiritual and in this galaxy
you've become the most unique star

She bathed me
When we were done I held her close
And asked every question my
wondering thoughts provoked
Until you drifted off in to the most
peaceful sleep that I had ever seen
A lover's screen play for the ages
End Scene.

# THE OUTRO

If you've gotten to this point one of two things happened. Either you're one of those people that flips to the end of the book just to see how long it is and this caught your eye or, you actually read the book and you're at the end (I hope you enjoyed it by the way). Either way you're here and either way I appreciate you in the utmost way. Some are probably wondering why it's so short and for some, this is the perfect length to fill/feed your soul. At this very moment I'm resisting the urge to over explain the length and the content in attempt to just let this be what it is. Although this is the end of the contents of this book, I added a few notes pages just to give readers a chance to digest and jot down their ideas feelings and whatever else comes to mind while reading. Once again, thank you for reading, whoever you are.

## THE END

May peace and love forever find its
way back to your heart…

# NOTES

## NOTES

# NOTES

# NOTES

www.ingramcontent.com/pod-product-compliance
Lightning Source LLC
Chambersburg PA
CBHW032102040426
42449CB00007B/1156